Another Last Summer

I0617388

Jaque Reed

Dedication

I dedicate this book to my dear granddaughter, Lily, who says she does not care for poetry. I tell her it's like falling in love — she just hasn't met the right one yet.

Here I am, even at my very advanced age, at it again. It's as if all my poems are already there … backed up inside me like hens' eggs, just waiting for the right time to pop out. I end up putting them together, really hoping that someone, somewhere will like them.

I've added two short stories as well because I didn't know what else to do with them. They began as poems, but turned themselves into prose, and I included them in this collection because they looked lonely, sitting there by themselves. I hope you like them too.

I am stepping into the river again. Heraclitus was right. It's not the same. I guess that's a good thing, isn't it?

Table of Contents

Another Last Summer

At the end of each August,
I tell myself, sadly,
"this will be my last summer
in the north woods."
Yet over and over, here I am,
well into my 90s.
Four of the other elders
have moved on.
The rest of us
can feel ourselves slowly peeling
away from this lifetime,
into the sweetly beckoning unknown.
Still, we continue to come.
Drawn by the invisible tug
of deep green moss
and birches hanging gracefully
over a placid lake.
Drawn by fierce thunderstorms
that cut the power
and leave us in candlelight.
Drawn by meadows of blueberries
and wild asparagus
in the early spring.

Loons call to each other
from across the lake,
mingling with the sound of canoe paddles
dipping quietly along the shoreline.
The shrieks of young cousins at play and
the scent of new balsam tips
drift through our dreams
Yes, we will all return:
tumbling children,
rumbling fathers,
grumbling grandparents,
and the mothers
intent on smoothing, healing
and keeping the peace.
Six generations
of forest lovers.
Of course, we will be back
even when none can see or hear us.
We will return and slip like otters
into the cool lake,
dance down the deer trails,
and never tire.
Don't we all know
there will never be a last summer?

Two Birds in a Forest

Sitting on a hummock of moss
beneath the elderly white pine,
with half-closed eyes
I gaze out at a meadow
afloat with daisies,
all holding still in the noonday sun.
I am listening to two birds
conversing with lyrical intensity
from different parts of the forest.
I close my eyes to better eavesdrop
on their spirited conversation.
What are their silvery notes telling each other?
Or asking?
Are they discussing newly flown fledglings?
Trying to decide where to have lunch?
Or maybe, plaintively, trying to renew a friendship
lost somewhere in flight.
At any rate, after sending their sweet couplets
along the gentle breezes,
in and among the fluttering poplar leaves,
one of them falls silent.
The other, after trying repeatedly to reconnect,
Is silent as well.
The silence rings out through the treetops,
and I sing my way home.

Rivers Are Forever

Down the river,
the small boat putters ahead
into yesterday.
Half-submerged roots
of ancient, fallen trees
make filigreed gates
into the future.
Water lilies spread out from the banks,
leaving a narrow center pathway
for slow moving travelers
heading
from one part of the past to another.
There is no now.
It is all now.
A log is lined with disinterested turtles,
a pointed stick of driftwood
sharply turns its head,
and flaps away
without a sound.
Heron …
A stand of hemlock
nods in recognition.

For no reason
I hum to myself,
"Mary had a little lamb."
It is grand to have no particular reason,
no particular destination,
just one splendid circle of primeval being,
following the current
into forever.

Forest Meeting

Large and mangy,
obviously no youngster,
he stood sideways
across the path
and stared,
without rancor
or fear.
With only a modicum of curiosity,
he seemed totally at ease.
Nevertheless, I was not tempted
to move forward.
I stood still, recalling
the various techniques to survive
an encounter with a bear.
"Make yourself large."
"Make yourself small."
"Don't make eye contact."
"Don't turn your back."
"Don't climb a tree—
he can climb better than you."
Why not simply treat him
with ordinary respect?
"Would you mind taking another route?"
I asked, in what I considered
a very reasonable tone.

He did not hesitate,
and obligingly ambled off into the trees,
giving me one last look over his shoulder,
leaving me with the melancholy feeling
that I had just had an unexpected encounter
with a long-lost cousin
that I would never meet again.

Summer Storm

Somewhere, from another lake,
just beyond the horizon,
we hear the threatening rumble—
marching boots
of an advancing army
intent upon invading our peaceful evening.
Warning banners flash
across the suddenly darkening sky,
and friendly biscuit clouds
turn angry, stomping out the sunset
in their churning confusion.
We put down our dinner forks
to listen and watch,
as a million tiny soldiers
blend themselves into a solid wall,
flinging themselves against the windows
in a furious, silvery mass.
Wind rises,
shrieking through the pines.
They bend in humility
but do not break.
The house grumbles and complains
but remains steadfast.
We wait for the lights to go off.
And they do.

They always do.
It takes only a few minutes
for nature's tantrum
to sweep on to rile and roil another lake,
leaving behind its slippery footprint,
while the sunset
takes up where it left off,
sliding gently down behind the tree line.
Birds return to finish their bedtime songs,
a squirrel pops out from under the deck,
and gives himself a shake.
Heavy drops
weigh down the birch leaves
and sparkle in the last of daylight.

How beautiful we are in the candlelight.

Brief Encounter

I did not notice him at first,
not even the slightest tickle,
as he made his slow pilgrimage
down the length of my hand and back.
With his thread-like proboscis,
he explored each raised, blue vein
with scientific precision.
What was he learning about me?
What should I be learning about him?
How exquisite were his orange and black patterned
wings,
each one edged
with lines of asymmetrical white dots,
all of him as carefully wrought
as a window of stained glass.
Thus, we studied each other
in those long, peaceful moments
that exist on the borders of time,
and I wondered
if I could bring him home,
just as he was,
on the back of my hand?
I had never had a butterfly as a pet.
He could play in the wildflowers
at the back of my house …

Just at that moment of conjecture,
the spell was broken.
Another identical winged creature
fluttered up,
making anxious circles
in the air above us.
"You naughty boy!
I've been looking everywhere for you.
Did you forget we are to have lunch together?
I've found a lovely pile of fresh deer poop for us."
And off they went,
side by side,
without a backward glance.
Old Sol was high in the sky now,
and I was aware of a latent rumbling
in my own stomach.
On the way home, I felt a certain regret
for the loss of my flighty friend,
but consoled myself with the thought
that my own noonday repast,
be it merely bread and cheese,
would be
in both flavor, texture and consistency,
far more appetizing
than his.

Tree/Me/We

The glorious greenness of you
I carry as well,
and the sap that runs through your hidden spaces,
each lightly-spinning leaf,
calls me sister.
When did I first notice that we share a mother?
That we entered this world
through the same vortex
of fire and water?
In a sun-kissed liminal space,
as I was close to sleep,
an unseen presence
brushed by quickly
leaving a few fibers
from a finely woven cloak
spreading along the back of my hand.
Threads of ancient wisdom that,
without announcing themselves,
worked their way
into the spaces around my heart
and built a nest.

Thus,
passing beneath your spreading branches,
feeling the deep hum

of your life-giving root system

tingling in the soles of my bare feet,
we gift each other
with a shored portion of eternity,
blessed by the universe,
and marked with our names
forever.

From the Edge

My lame foot
will not allow me
to drag it into the forest today,
so I hunker down at the edge
and listen to the trees
whispering to themselves
and to me.
"Soon," I hear them say, "soon."
I smell the balsam,
and the wintergreen.
I hear a woodpecker
pounding out his breakfast,
and some small somebody
rustling through the bracken.
I see the fragile poplar leaves,
twirling, silvery disks
in the light breeze.

There is a copper bell
ringing from somewhere
in the depths of green.
It calls forth an echo in my own heart.
"Come home," it calls, "Come home to us."
The trees send back my answer:
Soon, soon, soon.

The Oaks

Our roots are ancient
and deep.
They reach the beating heart
of the planet.
Our branches hold hands
in the last rays
of the sun,
breathing out life
and sharing our souls.

Guard us well,
you who love us,
and beware.
Beware the heedless ones,
with their hard, heavy plans
and disconnected hearts.
Beware of the tomorrow
after tomorrow,
for when we are gone,
so is hope.

Advice To a Child of the Earth

Move lightly in your moccasins,
that no tell-tale twig may snap beneath your feet.
Listen to the spirit whispers,
and follow your totem.
Play sweetly on your flute
and call forth a new dawn.
Beat softly on your drum,
but let its message be clear.
Take from the land
only what it can spare.
When you speak, let it be with kindness
and words of wisdom.
May your songs
spring forth full-throated from your heart.
That those in need of strength and comfort
may gather near.
Paddle your canoe with strokes straight and firm.
Look ahead, not behind.
Lie down at night with love,
and embrace the moon.
Rise up and greet the dawn with strength and purpose.
Live from the depths of your being
that you may lead your tribe wisely and well.
And when the days gifted by your creator
have come to an end,

fling your final song
skyward,
with equal measures
of joy and gratitude.

Inspired by the Lac Du Flambeau Ojibwe Tribal Museum

Little Drifter

I never noticed
how far I walked.
My feet went their own solid way,
following no path but their own,
deep and deeper into the wizardly greenness.
They came looking for me,
those wise grownups.
"Don't ever go so far from home!"
they scolded.
And I replied, wide-eyed,
"but I am home."

The Mother Tree

The wind moves gently
in and out of her topmost branches
with a hushed harmony of content.
Her wide overstory
provides a dappled canopy
for seedling offspring
and their companions.
Murmurings, cracklings,
tender greenlings reaching for the sun.
This is the world we perceive
on our forest ramblings.
But, oh what a busy life lies pulsing below!
A vast fungal network is weaving a tapestry,
reaching the taproot
with tiny, persistent tendrils,
providing a network of corridors
to those who call out
with small moist voices.
The Mother Tree hears.
The Mother Tree acts.
And through these fungal pathways sends
life in many nourishing forms
to her needy neighborhood.

This is where green is composed.
Out of the woven underlife,
forest villages connect.
This is how the forest endures
through all its mighty tribulations,
slowly building upon the loving care
of its many mothers.
So, we who tread the tangled pathways above
searching for our own source of strength and abundance,
where do our own networks lie?
If we should close our eyes,
then open them with a deeper, more focused gaze,
we might just become aware
that our mother tree is hiding
in plain sight.

Different Voices

In my sun-lit daze on the end of the dock,
from the depths of the lake,
I hear them.
Voices, I mean.
Quite different from the tender murmurs of the forest
carried on light breezes through the air.
Sometimes there are deep, buzzing sounds
rather like old men on a distant porch
discussing inclement weather,
the price of lumber, or
where the walleyes are biting.
I cannot pick up the words,
only sleepy tones of contentment,
and a sense
of many yesterdays
blending into today.
Other times, children are laughing,
chasing through the lily pads
with bubbles of joy.
Am I one of them?
Is this a part of the same yesterday?

On quieter days,
when the lake holds a shimmer of heat,
there is only one song,
slightly beyond my hearing
but leaving traces of melody.
It is telling me something
in its breathy sweetness,
guiding me somewhere …
but something
breaking into this timeless zone,
always snaps the faint connection.

A boat coming in to dock,
the sudden splash of an unruly wave,
a horsefly
and understanding escapes into the clouds,
leaving faint vibrations in its wake.

Thin spaces of the wild
are always singing out,
creating new patterns out of old harmonies.
Somehow, it makes no difference
that I do not understand the lyrics.

Summer's End

The wind blows hard from the north today.
A coven of angry witches
rages through the tree tops,
shrieking their incantations
against the season's change.
In the fireplace, pointy-headed gnomes
dance with glee,
and send up swirling messages
to the spirit of the weather,
"Do your best out there,
we will keep her warm anyway!"
In my imagination, I hear double-pitched wolf calls,
summoning the pack together for the winter.
I remember those haunting, chanting sounds
from a time, long ago,
when wolves ran free,
and their lairs were safe
from the killing-men.
I am almost too comfortable
in my old flannel shirts,
and ragged pants.
My hair has grown so much
that when I eat,
it sometimes catches in my mouth.

It will soon be time to go home.
But where is home?
And who am I when I am in it?
The forest whispers, "stay …"
Perhaps some day, some compelling day,
I shall simply drift off,
between the two tallest birches
that stand like sentinels
at the gateway
of the primeval.
So through the bracken and the brambles
I will travel
into the valley of bluebells,
finding my true home,
among the wise caretakers of the forest floor.
So why not today?

Heart Born to Wander

All her life she has been called
by soft, insistent whisperings
of unseen worlds beyond imagining.
All her life she has felt beckoning fingers
coaxing her further into the unmapped,
just beyond the boundaries of reality.
So she has wandered
forests, beaches, mountains,
and even city parks,
searching out what lies around corners,
what appears through the fine scrim
laid across the stage of everyday life.
What is it peering out from between
the tangled tree roots
with such tiny, twinkling eyes?
What hums beneath the bracken
that rings the pond
hidden deeply in the forest?
What dances in the mist
curling along the seashore?
Does she hear the low, prophetic voices
of rocks embedded in the mountainside?
They offer three million years of wisdom
to those who will stop and listen.

Does she long to set her feet upon the pathway
that sunset has painted across the lake?

All shimmers,
just a fingertip out of reach,
and soft bells ring out,
muffled in cloud banks
too dense to pierce.

And when her aging feet
can no longer carry her
to the far away and beyond,
she will seek out a sunny corner of her garden,
and continue to explore the wild spaces
in her own heart.

Duet

The essence of silence does not come
from quieting sounds around us,
but from quieting sounds within.
Through the stillness
come songs from a new source,
built upon half-remembered harmonies.
The hushed lyrics tell
of greening and renewal,
of walking barefoot on a mossy trail,
and noting the peeling of the birch,
and the pungent balsam tips
of new beginnings.
An old stump is rotting away,
gifting the forest floor
with hallowed nourishment.
Small frogs frolic in a puddle
that will soon be dry.
None of this is the silence
that you and I think we know.
This silence is teeming with sacred wisdom,
This silence hums with expectation.
This silence cannot help but sing,
and our hearts cannot help but answer.

Both/And

How beautiful is the candle flame
when seen through a veil of tears.
As I sit on the park bench,
a chill wind lifts the ends of my hair
and my nose begins to numb.
Still, the sun is warm and comforting on my knees.
Hip joints ache a bit,
but my lungs are filled with fresh, kelpy sea air
containing fragments of yesterday and today.
Above, the mountains pulse with ancient wisdom,
ignoring the darkness that gathers in their shadow.
The scaly, leafless branches of a lone sycamore reach out,
offering unconditional grace.
The path ahead is blurred,
obscured by doubts and anxiety,
but shimmering beyond our line of sight,
its tremulous notes barely heard,
is the beckoning song
of a silver-throated bird.

Tea Time
(Inspired by a Suggestion of Thich Nhat Hahn)

How long can I make my tea last?
Can it really take an hour to drink a cup of tea?
Will past and future dissolve in its milky depths,
and leave the purity of the present
shimmering on the surface?
Will I notice that the tea has gone cold?
If so,
will I even care?
Will it matter in the sweetness of now?
I can rest at last.
Without time,
neither fear nor regret
will have any place
to call home.

Do You Remember?

Do you remember
when life was a wild child
dancing in the rain?
Do you remember running on the beach
until you dropped?
Singing yourself hoarse
around a driftwood fire?
Do you remember dancing until daybreak
with a man you never saw again?
Do you remember rattling through rural France
in a rickety Renault?
Climbing a Mexican pyramid
with bits of ancient stone
crumbling away under your feet?
Do you remember the piercing excitement
of being chased by lightning bolts
down a forest path?
What a thrill to outrun a storm!

Do you remember the pain and the joy of passion,
the satisfaction of love fulfilled in flesh?
Do you remember happiness?
Or have you, as so many,
learned to live without it,
and find your solace
in one moment
of full-throated birdsong?

A Blessing of Crows

It is that lonely time of day,
when dark presses slowly down
and offers no way back.
It is the time of day when I am most conscious
that there is no more "we,"
simply me.
I sit at the window and watch
a murder of crows
gathering in the top branches
of what I call the talking tree.
How insistent they are
in their raucous conversations!
Sounding more like a protest meeting
than a simple accounting
of the day gone by—
Which picnic table has the tastiest crumbs?
Which angry old man came out in his pajamas
and threw stones at us?
Where is the coziest place to sleep tonight?

All at once, they rise in an untidy flurry,
edges billowing in and out,
still communicating with the same shrill jabber.
Not at all like a perfectly aligned wedge of geese,
whose destination is pre-set and purposeful,
never in doubt.
And yet, they hang together
in an undulating oneness.
Suddenly, mysteriously,
moving in one coherent body,
they wheel off and out of sight,
toward the low mountain range in the distance,
still talking, talking, talking,
still together.

The Other Side

What do you see
on the other side of the mountain?
Another mountain, of course,
humped and gray,
daring you to continue.
And so you keep on,
up one rock-strewn trail after another,
until finally,
when the tick-tock of time
has lost its urgency,
and your "to do" list lies
crumpled and ignored,
only then,
will you look down and see
the green valley of abundance,
for which every seeking heart yearns.
Each of us wanders different paths,
and finds different mountains to climb.
But when we come upon the last one,
and we stand breathless and drained,
the journey completed at last,
we find that the same valley
has been awaiting us all.

Uncoupled

We have paved over
our most ancient memories
of vast meadow space,
and the depths of the greenest forest.
They once spoke to us in a mother tongue.
Our soaring cathedrals
celebrate a name
but not a spirit.
We no longer hear messages
in the moving waters of a brook,
or heed the whisperings
of tiny things
that burrow.
We do not recall
the songs of our primal heartbeat,
nor can we sense throbbings of new growth
beneath our well-shod feet.
Our sight no longer expands
to see the universe
in a raindrop,
or a tear.
In our uncoupling from creation,
we have forgotten
what was once the baseline of our being.

What will it take for us to remember?
Must it be another birth?
And another dearth?

Young Mothers

Through the dense shrubbery
lining the creek bank,
I hear the soft strumming of a guitar.
A sweet, dream-like melody
drifting in—and through—
the Spring landscape,
like the voice of some strange
and prophetic sliver of birdsong.
Its harmonies call forth half-hidden memories
of tenderness and devotion.
When did I first own love like that?
Parting the spiky green leaves,
I make a space
through which I see,
at a distance across the creek,
an open meadow
and a group of young women
cradling their swaddled infants.
They sway gently
like willows in the breeze.
I close my eyes, becoming a willow myself,
and feel what it was once like
to be rocked, to be cherished,
to be held close to a beating heart.

In this moment on the fragile edge of time,
I am both mother and child,
nurturer and nurtured,
eternally at one with the universe.

Disneyland Lost:
A Prophecy

The gates of Disneyland have long been closed,
with streets dark and bare,
save for a few flickering ghosts
of faded phantasies.
The pirate's ship has sunk.
Cotton candy melted
into pink smears.
Mickey and Minnie hold hands,
bowing their heads in grief.
Outside, bright city lights still burn
and parties continue,
but the guests depart early,
leaving half-empty glasses
to make cloudy rings
on politely polished furniture.
While oceans continue to rise,
forests shrivel and shrink.
Birds in flight drop to earth
without a sound,
and unfed spiders
curl into tiny balls
quickly blown away
in the dusty wind.

The gates of Disneyland are closed,
long rusted tight.
But behind them,
drifting like random snowflakes,
can still be heard
the faint, prophetic strains of,
"It's a Small, Small World."

The Power of Song

If you whistle down
the back alleys of darkness,
chant through streets
both high and low,
strum your harp on hillsides
blooming with lupin,
let the pipings of a silver flute
travel from wave to wave
until they touch all shores,
allow the deepest vibrations of a cello
to echo in the lichen-clothed rocks,
then angel choirs will answer
with their own sweet anthems of joy.
If our own planet were steeped and enfolded
in the full divinity of music,
perhaps beady-eyed, sticky-fingered evil
would stop its sundering progress
and listen,
and feel
the haunting vibrations
that are born
in the music of Love.

Oak is Nice for a Man

Coffins …
I have never thought of them
in the plural before,
but here they are,
lining the cavernous showroom,
row upon row.
It could be any furniture warehouse.
Such a variety of boxes
for housing death!
Solid, heavy, reassuring us
that nothing can escape.
Heart-breaking tiny ones,
and extra-long …
for basketball players?
Quilted satin linings of muted colors,
winking brass fittings everywhere.
In one, there is even a telephone.
(Who do you call when you're dead?
God, I guess.)
My feet have left the floor,
I float somewhere in an in-between space.
My kind friend breaks into the fog,
"I always think oak is nice for a man."

Grateful for the prompt, I echo,
"Yes, oak is nice for a man.
I'll take that one.
can we go home now?"

Later, lying tearless,
in my too large, too empty bed,
behind closed eyelids I see
a boulevard of half-open caskets
stretching beyond the horizon,
while a thousand phones
ring on and on
into the indifferent night.

The Wrong Question

One New Year's Eve a friend asked,
"What have you done in your life you regret?"
A moment of thought …
and then,
"The things I most regret
are the things I have NOT done."
I did not play with the little red-headed girl
because I did not like red hair.
I did not feed the ragged old man
because he was dirty
and smelled.
I never noticed the hunger in his eyes
as he watched me eat my sandwich.
I did not respond to the oddly behaving woman
who lived across the street,
ignoring her need for compassion.
I regret the flowers brought to a dying friend
two hours late.
Yes, I am sorry for all the sunny days,
and preoccupied moments
when I have turned my head,
and walked on past,
or worse, never noticed
an outstretched hand,
a pleading eye,
a muffled whimper.

Their wraith-like images
rise up in shadowed moments
to pluck at my sleeve
and remind me
that with each self-satisfied oversight,
each eye misted with ego,
a snippet of my soul
dries up and blows away.

Afternoon Dream

In the distance,
do I hear a bentwood flute
playing notes not heard in this world?
Do I see colors
I cannot name?
Are those willows swaying in the breeze
or a troop of mothers
rocking their new born babes?
Did that speckled green frog
just wink at me,
and wave a tiny webbed hand?
This is one of those times of translucence
When shadows behind the veil
take form and dance their way
into my drowsy world.
I can see,
I can hear,
but I cannot touch.
Illusion and reality
blend and blur in the afternoon sun.
I swim somewhere
between two shifting landscapes.
Both are true.
Both are mine.
Both are forever.

Bell Tones

Some days I hear bells,
all kinds of bells.
They're not real, of course,
but I hear them just the same.
The scissor grinder pedals his bike
down a narrow city street
beneath our windows.
All the neighborhood ladies
run down with their scissors and knives,
and chat while he brings each blade to its sharpest
potential.
Riding on the golden Roman sunset,
deep cathedral bells
cross the sky
and echo off the ancient stones.
Clouds of swallows
swoop in and around the cupolas,
waiting for the mighty vibrations to fade,
when they can return to their nests
as if nothing had happened.

High above the Gulf of Mexico,
a tiny ice cream cart trundles
along the road beneath the cliff.
Its tuneful bell sings merrily,
"sailing, sailing, over the bounding main …,"
blending in with tropical sunshine
winking off the sea,
and the occasional leaping dolphin.
So far down …
all I can do is watch.

On another hillside
just over the horizon,
a small, white church
rings its bell hopefully.
I turn away with regret,
still searching for truth
that does not live in a box.
And then there is another sound
coming from a space deep within,
sometimes as distant as Russian troika bells
but always saying the same thing.
"It is time to write
another poem."
I ignore this summons at my peril.

Snail Tale

As a child,
I liked to step on snails
because of the squish
and the crunch.
Now with apprehension
I wonder,
in my sometimes heedless journey,
what else
have I trod upon
just to hear the crunch?

Temptation

If I pick the blossoms,
there will be no fruit.
If I wait for the fruit,
there will be no
lacy flowers
to scent
my cottage.

How unkind
to make me choose
between fragrance and flavor.

Once Upon a Town

Aunt Sally—
I think of it often,
that village in a park
designed in circles
instead of squares.
In the spring,
everywhere you go
smells of lilacs.
No one locks doors
or even remembers
where they hid the key.
Very few cars—
we walk everywhere,
and to go to the city,
if you must,
there is always the train.

In the long summer evenings,
we sit on our wrap-around porch
greeting the neighbors strolling by.
Sometimes I dream I am wandering
along the freckled sidewalks,
saying, "Hi there"
to everyone I once knew.

Could a town ever get to Heaven?
If it could be there
just waiting for me,
I sure would be happy.

Duck—

It's all mine,
This nice little pond,
slippery, muddy, weedy.
Full of fat little things to eat.
Up on the hill above
is a house full of books,
(whatever they are—paper things.)
I see the children come and go.
They bring some in,
they take some out.
Sometimes they stay awhile.
I see them turning pages
as they sit in the big window.
How content they seem …
but I think to myself
how much better off I am
than those dry little creatures.
I love my wetness,
my mud,
my small town pond,
my Heaven.

Two Little Girls—

In the summertime,
we sit under the big apple tree
having a tea party with our dolls.
The grass is so nice and green,
and there are birds everywhere.
We have enemies, though.

They are called "the Dopeydopes"
and sometimes they hide in the tree
and fly down to steal our dolls,
but we stamp our feet
and yell at them,
and they run away.
Who's afraid of a few stupid Dopeydopes?

We used to live in the city.
It was pretty dirty
and noisy too,
like buses and sirens and stuff.
This is way better.
I can't think of any place I'd rather live
except Oz, maybe.
I don't suppose even Heaven can be much better.

Ida—
I cook for white people
in a big white house.
They give me three dollars a week.
Not much,
but I make do.
Today, through the kitchen door,
I saw two little girls
under the apple tree,
having a tea party with their dolls.
I remember how much I wanted a pretty doll,
but we didn't have money for a doll,
so Mama made me one
out of scraps of aprons and stuff.

One arm was longer than the other,
but I loved her anyway.
One day a lady give me a nice piece of lace.
I made it into a collar,
and wear it to church every Sunday.
Preacher says that Heaven will be full of pretty things,
kind of like this town
would be if I could live here.

George—

Yes sir! This is a really fine town!
We made a good choice, Edith and I,
deciding to live here,
and now our grandchildren are here too.
Only one thing, though,
there have been a lot of newcomers lately.
People with long, funny names
that come from a place called Bohemia.
They don't dress like us,
and they don't act like us.
Edith says we shouldn't mind.
Because they live on the other side of town.
But what if one of them decided to move next door to us?
Well, we'd just have to move out, that's all.
And wouldn't that be a shame?
Because we always said this little village
was a piece of Heaven.

Edith—

Oh George, you're such a snob!
Some of those people are perfectly nice.
For instance,
there is Mrs. Smaha
who owns the only beauty parlor in town.
When her husband was so sick,
I put my arms around her,
and told her I would do anything I could to help.
Then I sent over some good, healthy soup.
Of course, I could never
invite her to one of my luncheons.
She would feel so out of place…
still, I count her as a friend.
But, oh George, why are you such a snob?

Lilacs in the Rain—

As lilacs droop lower and lower in the late spring rain,
and a train whistle crawls across the night sky,
thousands of miles away
an old woman turns in her bed
and remembers
a village on the river,
and:
The roar and click
of roller skates on an uneven side walk,
popsicle juice running down the inside of her wrist,
a library, warm and welcoming,
shelf after shelf
promising magical kingdoms.

A bicycle parade on the Fourth of July.
The deep, heavy bong of a school bell.
Her kindly uncles,
their pockets jingling with small change.
Joyful expectations of a Saturday morning—
out the door, and away on her bike,
in search of the yellow brick road.
The low growl of roller skates
has long been silenced,
the bike path along the river,
overgrown.
The dim, cozy library
is bright with florescent lights now,
and the pragmatic knowledge
of a dozen computer screens.
The uncles in their three piece suits
have moved on
to jingle their quarters
in another realm.
But the lilacs have never faded,
as she readies herself for her final adventure.
Their scent, remains washed in April rains,
still singing their songs of promise.
They will guide her gently
past the steeples and domes,
and all the concrete monuments to fame,
to that landscape outside of time,
that lives forever,
just over the rainbow.

Dark Memories

The heavy darkness enfolds her
with its filmy phantoms,
and their sinister, unspoken threats.
She tries hiding her head under the pillow,
but night demons do not relent.
How comforting is her mother's bed
with the fragrant silk of her nightgown,
and the warmth of soft arms.
What safety lies in a cuddle,
and an embrace that lasts the night.
But this time, Mother says
(not unkindly),
"you're too old for this now,
go back to your own bed."
The man beside her rolls over
but does not wake.
The child within still remembers
how cold the floor felt
beneath her bare feet
as she padded back to her small room
where the hobgoblins awaited her return
with fearsome glee.

Summer Morning

Sweet dew is still cool upon the grass.
Hollyhocks along the fence
turn their faces
toward the re-born sun.
From across a meadow can be heard
the gentle lament of a mourning dove
in its slow, measured paces.
On the second-to-last porch step,
sits a small girl with unbrushed hair,
heart cradling an ache too deep for tears.
She stares at a narrow road outside the gate
until her eyes begin to blur.
"Maybe today will be the day he comes home."
The dove answers her tenderly,
"Oh no, never … never … never."
The child turns, and moves slowly back into the house
to find her cornflakes and milk.

Later …
I wish that they had told me he was dead.
I knew about death.
I had seen dead birds, dead beetles, dead frogs.
I knew there was no return.
But they kept coming up with appropriate euphemisms.
"Your Daddy's in Heaven now." (Where was that?)
"Your Daddy's with the angels." (Who were they?)
"Your Daddy's in a better place"
(What could be a better place than home, here with
me?")

So still, even at my advanced age, I look for him.
In my deepest REM sleep,
he skirts around corners, not even casting a shadow.
He leaves parties before I arrive.
The more quickly I move toward him,
the more quickly he disappears.
All I want is to hug him one more time
and remind him that when he left for that better place,
he forgot to say "Goodbye."

What is Holy?

A blade of grass
trampled under my heedless foot,
springs back when I have passed,
to stand tall again in the light.
A family of raindrops soaks the thirsty soil
and stirs long dormant seeds with hope.
Dark, foggy fingers lift one by one,
from across the sleepy hilltops,
that their slopes may greet the sun
one more day.
Is this not holy?
Are these not spectacular moments of grace?
Can holiness be found in a bishop's mitered hat
or stately stride down the aisle?
Or in silver goblets awaiting on the altar?
Is it found in the fragile wafer
blessed by the hand of a priest
and melting on my tongue?
Holiness cannot be conferred.
Holiness hovers sweetly in the air,
waiting for us to notice
and stretch out our arms.
Holiness is the offering and the partaking
of love without boundaries.
Our church cannot be holy
until we are.

Chicago Snow

With such delight
we welcome it—
That first soft snowfall.
Children run outside
to catch the flakes on their tongues,
and hurry to the park
to build lopsided snowmen.
The stumpy fire hydrants
bundled with white fluff,
stretch out their stubby arms,
and welcome us to magic.
Bells ring out on street corners.
Christmas is coming.
Snow is still a symbol of purity.
Cold settles in
and takes up residence
in our bones,
as winter grinds on
with heavy, plodding feet.
The frigid wind
carries sharp, gritty fragments
from all parts of the city.

We slant ourselves against its fury
with mufflers tight across our mouths,
not daring to look up
to meet the ferocious eye
of this most bitter season.
Old snow gathers on street corners
in sooty heaps,
striped with the yellow offerings
of small, leashed dogs.
Trees etch their black branches
across a stone sky.

One day of pale sunshine,
the ragtags of winter
begin to lose their grip.
Air carries a new softness,
and the scent of something hopeful.
One by one, pink tulips
open in the park,
and buds plump
on cold, bare branches.
We go to our beds smiling,
looking forward to a new, embraceable season.
Awakening in the morning,
our smiles take on an ironic twist,
tricked again!

As we slept in happy anticipation,
tough old winter had not let us off the hook,
but taken his hoary hand
and shoved gentle spring
back into the grave.
Another six inches of snow
covered all the new, green beginnings.

We are disappointed,
but not disheartened,
for all of us know
that spring,
like the grace of God,
always appears
when we need her most.

The Thinking Trap

Stepping up on the bus,
out of the February slush,
she takes brief note
of the passengers,
each encased in a brooding bubble,
unfocused, staring straight ahead,
as indifferent as turtles on a log.
Her entrance makes not the slightest ripple
in their formless self-containment.
In the dry, overheated air,
frayed ribbons of discontent
circle around her head briefly,
then drift away on a current of air
from the suddenly opened door.
"I think I left water out for the dog—
can't remember …
Losing it?"
"I hope the boss-man is in a better mood today.
Whatever made me take this dumb job, anyway?"
"Why did he just walk out on me like that?
What did I do wrong?
Maybe I should have learned to play bridge like he
wanted.
Maybe I should have lost those ten pounds …"

"Why didn't that damn mechanic fix my car on time?
Now I have to ride this crappy bus
like any other loser."

"Oh my Lord, he's so sick,
and the doctors aren't helping!
I just pray our insurance holds out."
"God, I need a drink!
It's so fuckin' hard to hang on,
maybe I just won't.
Bars open at eleven around here.
Maybe just one wouldn't hurt …"
"Stole money from Ma's purse again.
Well, she owes me, the old bitch!"
"Geez, it's snowing again.
I hate snow.
I hate this crummy city.
I want to go home
where the sun shines once-in-a-while."
"I was glad when she died,
I thought, 'Now I don't have to listen
to her screech at me anymore.
I sure looked stupid in that old black suit,
pretending to wipe my eyes.
I wish I could just kick the bucket too,
and get the whole thing over with …'
Oh Bessie, what will I ever do without you?"

She gets off the bus before her stop,
and standing on the street corner,
tips her head back,
letting the clean, newly falling snow
settle gently on her tongue.

Holy Silence

Through a wide-open door,
sun sets on a rose garden.
A light breeze stirs the leaves,
but no petals fall.
Shadows spread in long fingers,
resting gently on the unresisting grass.
The distant drums of the past
are silent,
and no ram's horn
heralds the future.
This moment of holy silence hangs
in no-time, no-space,
and I, the watcher, have
no name, no me-ness,
only the sweet mysterious freedom
of being.
Is this what they call Mercy?
Or is it death,
caught in a dream
outside of time?
Perhaps they are one and the same …
And, if so,
how many times
have I died?

In The Midst of Life

With the rictus of death
he grinned at me
from the bottom
of a 20-foot cross.
All up and down the wrought iron façade
were religious symbols,
each one delicately crafted.
The original serpent
winding itself gracefully
around a slender tree trunk,
Jacobs's ladder
heading heavenward,
a dagger-pierced heart
balanced at the top.

All enchanted me,
except for the grim
skull and crossbones
facing me at the foot.
I wore a mask like that
one Halloween.
It was meant for terror,
not comfort.

"Must you remind us of what lies at the end?
Everyone stripped to his bony container?"
I asked him.
His mocking grin only grew wider.
Then I noticed
that his hollow eyes
were clogged with sticky cobwebs,
and there was dirt between
each and every one of his even teeth.
His bald head was dull,
and speckled with tiny bits
of everyday debris.
Death was attacking death.

I took a damp cloth
and gently wiped out
the deep eye sockets,
cleaned carefully between each tooth,
and polished his head
until it shone
with a soft glow
in the late afternoon sun.

As I stood back
to assess the results
of my unexpected task
(call it tending death?)
the menacing grin
became a loving smile
of acceptance,
and I smiled back at my new friend,
Death.

Jaque Reed at St Mark's In-the-Valley Episcopal
Church

"Blessed Are the Poor in Spirit,
for Theirs is the Kingdom of Heaven"

Matthew 5:3

Who are they, the poor in spirit?
And where does their poverty lie?
The poverty springs forth from the restless ache
of love not quite fulfilled,
of atonal harmonies
hovering lightly on wandering pathways
that have forgotten their final destination.
It dwells in the softly beating heart
of a dying bird.
It stirs a wanderer to become a seeker
after the Balm of Gilead,
to climb the rock-strewn mountain
for a glimpse of the hidden side,
to find the source of songs
only half heard,
and the sweetest, purest of waters,
still to be tasted.
The seeker yearns after promises
as yet unfulfilled.

But still circling the universe.
The poor in spirit long for meaning,
and to catch the urgent, piercing call
of the kingdom that beckons
through the mists
from the other side of the mountain.
A call that begs an answer.
A call that once heeded,
fills the empty spaces
surrounding every needy heart.

What Lies Between

Following the flow of crimson
that moves with gentle stealth
behind my closed eyelids,
there is a murkiness
as another color seeks to make its way
into the spectrum.
Shot with winking sprinkles of gold,
a density of green slowly appears—
a thick, leafy forest
transforms itself into vibrant, translucent
emerald.
I want to rest in it …
Forever.
But, bit by bit, the green is overtaken
by pulsing, shape-changing forms
of gold-fringed violet
dancing across a midnight background.
The figures fade in and out,
bearing messages of truth
beyond my understanding.
I long to join them
in their graceful patterns,
but they melt off.
A star falls.

Now there is only a solid expanse of white …
Not the white of freshly fallen snow,
nor yet the white of sudden sea spray,
nor that of a nesting swan.
It is only the white of nothingness,
around me
like a mother's arms.

Though it is seen quite clearly
with another pair of eyes,
in the vast sweep of nothing
are planted
the blessed and terrifying seeds
of all that is,
and all there ever
will be.

The Word of God

It is a hard climb up the mountain.
Her pockets are weighted with problems.
It takes a day and a night
to rise above the buzz and hum, the rumble and roar
of planetary being.
When she gets to the top,
she holds out her arms,
"Oh God help me."
God answers,
"Don't bother me now, child,
I'm busy."
Busy? Busy doing what?"
"Busy creating."
"But you did that long ago,
and in six days, too.
What are you creating now?"
"I'm creating you,"
says God.

Another Advent

1.
It was an odd place
to expect a desert flower to bloom—
the living room
of a cramped New York apartment.
The four of us,
longtime friends,
knowing that it was ready for its hallelujah opening,
gathered around it
in a long night vigil.

It was a time of deep connection
between us and an opalescent flower
about to be born.
The love, palpable,
throbbed like a Bach concerto.

As we held our breath,
the petals began to unfurl,
and a pale blossom
of fragrant purity faced us,
inviting us into its heart.

We moved off to bed,
silently, trancelike.
In the morning, the flower was gone,
petals scattered on the floor,
but the blessed message it carried
never faded,
and even after fifty years,
we continue to hold it close,
and continue to live in the hope
of what is yet to be.

2.
As on another night,
with the shepherds to keep vigil,
the angels sang on the dark hills
behind the little town of Bethlehem,
"Hallelujah … Peace on Earth."
They, too, were gone in the morning,
their message of a miracle birth
still ringing through time.

We carry its music in the corners of our hearts,
and through a world bristling with drawn swords
we remember a pearly white flower
quietly unfolding into the night,
and await another blossoming—
another promise,
not yet kept.

Hands

As we stand in our circle,
holding hands,
passing on the sweet energy
of love and compassion,
we sway slightly
to some inner rhythm.
And a voice from another sphere
bids us to keep in mind,
that the hand that gives,
and the hand that receives,
belong to the same body.

A Letter to the Episcopal Church

When I think of religion,
I am put in mind
of dusty corners, a hint of bluish mold,
and the dregs of red wine.
Why don't you open those heavy, stained-glass windows,
casting their purple shadows over our drowsy faces,
and let in the scent of summer clover,
or the biting wonder of new-fallen snow?
Why don't you retire those dragging Victorian dirges,
and blend the sound of honeybees
with gentle lament of the mourning dove?
Could you not
move away those creaking nail-studded doors
that close so firmly with a dull thud,
separating all within from all without?
Could not your ushers welcome
new thoughts, new hopes, new dreams,
and bid them take their seats among the dominions
of ten thousand yesterdays?

Please, old friend,
take heed to the newly-cleansing light
that clamors to make a home in your heart,
and let it expand into your deepest understanding.
For its beams carry full-throated joy,
and in its joy lie new Truths
fashioned to serve us all
as we enter
a darker tomorrow.

Lenten Reflections

Encounter With a Fallen Star

The wide, oddly shaped puddle
reflects another world.
A world of faintly rippled distortions,
and vague contrasts.
I see the church doors,
wavering indistinctly across the troubled surface,
and somewhere from a high place,
a disappointed star
is falling
falling
falling,
still clutching a slowly fading torch.

"Stand Up to the Devil and He Will Turn and Run"

I recognized him right away,
on that day of forked lightening,
and plunging indecisions.
Before he had a chance
to bite off a piece of my soul,
I commanded him to do
something anatomically impossible,
and ran out the back door
into holy sunshine,
congratulating myself
on my lucky escape—
little realizing
that he was sitting there smirking
right under my favorite
apple tree.

Holy Waiting

On this Holy Saturday when the world between worlds
holds its breath,
I am sitting in my garden
simply waiting.
Waiting for seeds to burst open,
bulbs to rise up from the ground
in their full glory,
a painted butterfly
to hover just above the wobbly fence,
and Jesus, the Christ,
to come forward down the path
with outstretched arms,
smiling at death.

The Downward Eye

Her troubled mind
plays with the wilted petals
of yesterday
while, unnoted,
riots of midsummer daisies
bless the hillsides
of today.

The Place of Being

As age has put a firm hand
on my shoulder,
I find that doing
interferes with my being,
so I sit in my garden
catching the last rays
of the sun,
in my faded apron,
and giving the glory to God.

Distraction

Some days I am
a two dimensional silhouette
dancing across a blank wall.
Not real,
even to myself.

Advice to Myself

You who seek so earnestly after Truth,
know that you, also,
are being sought.
Rest in your own garden,
and allow yourself
to be found.

Survival

The frog songs are late this year,
as is spring itself.
The chill fog has come snaking down the hillsides
every day,
an invading army of stealth
stinging our cheeks with its tiny needles.
Spring bides its time,
not defeated,
but delayed.
The frogs have decided to wait no longer.
A creek side chorus of troubadours
send their tempting invitations
across the valley.
"Ladies, we are the best,
the strongest,
the healthiest.
We can give you hundreds
of pop-eyed progeny.
Come to us,
come to us!"
So please, dear lady frogs,
heed these urgent calls,
belated or not.
Hop on down to the creek,
and choose your ideal mate.

Continue to populate your world,
as it belongs to us all,
and we two-legged creatures
are slowly realizing that
when you begin to disappear,
so will we.

Cloud City

Behind and above the slowly greening foothills,
a billowy wall of cloud houses is being built
far away and near at the same time.

How delightful—
a condominium where myriad balconies
look out over the world,
a steeple from which I can almost
hear a deep summoning bell,
a fairytale castle, complete with turrets,
and a moat.
And here is one I really like.
A peaky roofed cottage
with lacy curtains.
Is that a picket fence too?
(I wonder how long it would take to get there …)

While I stand pondering
what I would need for the journey,
the wind picks up,
the city begins to roll sideways,
and—as do so many dreams—
breaks into shreds and snippets
floating off into the unknown.

The last thing to go is the picket fence.

Rabbit Umveldt*

In the soft buzz of late afternoon sun,
I close my eyes.
When I open them,
at some mysterious prompt,
there he is—
sitting motionless,
not two feet away,
staring at me with a fixed gaze.
No, not truly staring at all,
as his eyes are blank,
focused no higher than my kneecap.
Instead, he is exploring me with his nose,
each nostril doing a little twitching dance
like partners in an Irish jig.
It takes a moment or two for him to decide
that I am neither dangerous nor edible,
and off he hops
to make a leisurely inspection of my garden.
My immediate relevance in his world of survival
seems to have passed,
leaving a slight shift in my consciousness.
Probably none in his.
Away he goes,
flattening himself under the fence
without a backward glance,

having eaten nothing but a few fallen rose petals.
If he should decide to return, some other sleepy
afternoon,
perhaps he could manage to twitch himself
more into the me-ness of me,
and together we could find a different nourishment
of value far beyond
any petal abandoned in the mud.
*immediate environment

Am I Real Yet?

Throughout this life,
I have gone
from me to me,
discarding the worn-out ones
behind on the trail
like empty juice cartons.
I still ask,
"Who am I, really?"
Am I only a pinch
of a stranger's imagination,
flickering Northern Lights
across a dark, frozen horizon,
or a cat scampering across a TV screen?

What is it that will make me real?
And how will I know
when it happens?

The answer comes from elsewhere,
from someone who follows my careless steps
with great patience
along the trail of confusion.
I hear
a voice like wind through the treetops.

"When you are worn and frayed at the edges,
lumpy from so many hugs,
when you find yourself
so full of love
that the golden light of it
shimmers through your fingertips,
and your smile
melts the frost
of defeated hearts,
when joy purrs like a warm cat
curled in your heart,
when you know that you and your neighbor
have become 'we,'
then you will know
you are real,
without ever being told.
Then, after a lifetime of wandering,
you will know you are home at last."

Almost Purple

Good morning, poppy!
How did you get here,
so suddenly blooming
at my doorstep?
Did you arrive willy-nilly
on the spring breezes,
or have you been dozing,
barely underground,
waiting for the right rain,
the right sun,
the right love?

Why are you such a splendid tint
of not quite purple?
I love your delicately shaded petals,
leading the eye downward
to a thumbprint of aubergine
and a tiny coconut cake in the center.
It must be my birthday …

Have you gathered all the other colors,
borne on fractured fragments of light,
into your own being,
leaving behind this elegant almost-purple
as a gift for my early morning eyes?

How did you know it was just what I wanted—
just what I needed—
when I never even knew it myself?

Two Songs

The clouds have lifted
and fingers of dawn
begin to spread across the sky.
At the shifting edge of sand and water,
she begins her song to the sea,
a melody of longing unencumbered by words
and filled with the sweet yearning of time gone by.
The sea answers with its own song of remembrance.
Born in greeny depths
carried on the tide,
tossed upward by a rogue wave.
There is no blending of sounds here.
No grand musical medley.
Too much time has passed since they were one,
she and sea.
Too long has she walked the land
and breathed in otherness.
The songs drift along on parallel paths,
two birds
calling to each other
from different parts of the forest.

Finding the Way Home

All darkness is not dark—
it only seems so at first.
Slowly our eyes pick up dimensions,
vague outlines and shapes.
A lone star breaks through the cloud banks,
a small slice of moon
continues its well-planned journey
across the heavens.
This night was not like that.
The trail in the forest had become black,
suddenly and completely,
as if a thick cloak had been pulled over my head.
I was trapped in a darkness within darkness,
tensed, on the edge of panic.
Seconds later came the rain,
not in drops, but in solid sheets
turning the ground on which I was standing
into a primeval bog.
There was no question of moving
in any direction.
Time lost all meaning.
Then, with a strange sense of tenderness,
the opaque darkness opened its mouth
and swallowed me whole,
pulling me into its very being.

I was no longer afraid,
but absorbed into a comforting,
pulsating kernel of beginnings—
the birthplace of trust.
Standing immobile,
mud rising around my ankles,
I waited
without expectations,
for whatever would happen next.
As if rewarding me for my patience,
the storm sent a gift.
Jagged flashes of lightening,
coming every thirty seconds or so,
briefly lighted the narrow path
coaxing me to move forward cautiously,
two steps forward in the light,
one more in memory.
Then, stand still and wait.
All in good time,
the comfortable outline of the cabin
stood out in front of me.
I was returned to my own doorstep,
not through the dark,
but with the dark.
Not in the dark,
but of the dark,
where the steady white light
of a kerosine lamp in the window
welcomed us both home.

The Greatest Need

An odd part of aging is
how our needs seem to shrink
as our perspectives expand.
We need fewer shoes,
fewer purses,
fewer rings,
smaller homes,
smaller parties,
and maybe only a tiny dinner
in front of the TV.
Life is so much more comfortable
without a list of "must-haves."
However, there is one primal need that never fades,
remains basic to all that moves and breathes,
and follows us like a wisp of melody
in sunshine or thunderstorm
every day of our shrinking lives.
Without a true friend in our hearts,
we are unfinished puzzles
with gaping spaces waiting to be filled—
the picture longing to be completed.
A friend knows how to laugh
and to cry, not only with you,
but for you.

A friend will take pleasure in your goofiness,
joining in and loving you for it.
A friend knows your flaws,
but does not judge you for them.
In darker times, a friend will just show up
and ask, "How can I help?"

A friend knows what you need
before you know it yourself
(such as a salt cellar),
and it will be on your doorstep the next day.
A friend knows your deepest secret,
and keeps it tucked away.
A true friend is a drink of cool water
in a heat wave,
a soft teddy bear
frazzled from so many hugs,
the first star to come out at night
and the last to fade into the dawn.
How blessed it is to have such a friend
and how much more blessed it is
to be one.

Enclosed Spaces

The brightly beaded borders
of a restless imagination
capture ripples of unsung song.
They weave back and forth
like dappled koi
trapped in a small pond.
A lone bird
rides a current of wind
in a tiny patch of sky.
The haunted scent of honeysuckle
from a long-lost garden
tiptoes silently into my dreams.
It tickles.
In half a hospital room,
cluttered with odd necessities,
I travel,
as through a crystal,
into the mystery of smallness.
Into the veins
of a curled, brown leaf,
into the colors that live
in a sharp pinch of sand,
into the saltiness
of an unexpected teardrop,
that harbors enough love
to complete an entire world.

Getting There

Looking up from the twisting trail,
I see that all the scenery has changed.
New trees, new gardens,
new faces silently watch from unfamiliar windows.
Even the horizon is not what it was—
more splendid shades of color,
and somehow, nearer, clearer.
Am I still me?

The river I planned to cross
has changed its course.
The gleaming mountain ahead
has become a tropical valley.
Flowers pulse, zooming in and out of sight.
So, who am I when all around me has been replaced?

I am simply the same flawed being,
struggling to get from here to there,
not realizing that I have been "there" all along.

On the trail laid out by some mysterious hand,
there are no endings, only beginnings,
no tomorrows, only today,
no meaning, only being.

Shadow of a Crow

All the pretty trinkets are back in their boxes,
twinkling lights unplugged.
Altar candles burned down to a nub.
Carols of hope and glory folded safely away,
while truth slinks back into our lives.
Small clouds scuttle across the sky
like flocks of frightened sheep.

Thousands of miles across a restless ocean,
the cries of violated women circle the planet.
Along with the wordless keening
of parents holding their dead children
in a rubble-strewn street.
Their grief reaches us in the dark of night,
and we know not why we shiver
under warm blankets.

On one side of our nervous border,
masses of the desperate
travel in herds
through unwelcoming territory.
We too, will turn them away.

I live in two rooms and a garden.
I am warm and fed.
I drink milky tea and listen to Mozart.
Life is safe.
But just outside
a wayward crow
casts a long black shadow across my doorstep,
and disappears without a sound.

I stand at my window
waiting, as always,
for the light of the evening star.
to break through.

Night Visitor

Late last night
you slipped into my bed.
We greeted each other with wordless
cries of joy.
We lay wrapped together
until daybreak.
When my eyes opened
you were gone,
but the pillow beside me
held a smooth dent
and my cheeks still
tingled from your whiskery kisses.
I lay still for a long time
trying to balance the heavy bricks
of regret,
building a wall
around my heart.
Is this my penance
for loving you more
in death
than in life?

Private Epiphany

Is it the star that has stopped its passage,
or is it I?
What I thought I was following has,
instead, been following me.
Now its silver beam
no longer points to a path ahead,
but illuminates my own small garden,
as would a lantern
held aloft by a kindly hand.

At my feet lies a dirt-crusted treasure chest,
rusty-hinged,
dotted with half-hearted teeth marks
of a small animal that gave up too soon.

Remembering Pandora,
I hesitate.
Would I be better off not knowing what lies within?
What if a thousand angry insects swarm out
to harass and sting?
What if it is filled with shredded regrets of the past?
Worse yet, what if it is empty?
With a whine and a creak,
the lid slowly opens on its own.
With wonder, I stare into gently shifting mists.

My eyes struggle to adjust
as shapes form and reform from some hidden depth.
This is not something I have met before.

As mind consciousness begins to fade backwards,
the eye of the heart takes charge,
showing that the time of doing
is coming to an end,
and a time of being is beginning to reveal itself.
I shall keep the lid open
and wait in the peace of a beloved garden
until all there is,
is being.

Other Pathways

The pandemic has ended,
or so we are told …
but the world is not the same.
Nor do we quite recognize
our own small circles of being.
The universe has begun to unfold,
and in the creases
allows us to hear
new voices singing,
gives us a glimpse
of other pathways,
always present,
but hidden in the mysterious
Mobius strips of time.

How many are watching the unfolding?
How many are listening to the songs?

We need not be afraid of where we are going,
nor even of where we have been.
The great danger lies
in standing still,
and letting the final whimper
have its way.

Last Request

Time, in its merciless march,
seems to have asked only one thing of me—
that I endure.
And having done so for a great many years,
all I ask in return
is the time-ripened gift
of a perfect pear.

Short Stories

A Non-Fairy Tale

Almost all fairy stories begin with "Once upon a time", but there are no fairies in this story. It comes from that space beyond the curtain of reality, the land where dreams are born, and you must decide for yourself where truth and reality blend to make the story real for yourself.

So, we begin.

Once upon a time, on the edge of a vast, constantly whispering forest, there was a castle; and in this castle lived a young, very pretty princess who was wise beyond her twelve years of life. The princess spent her days watching from the window of a downstairs library; a room that only she ever entered. How she longed to escape the confines of the castle's stone walls and explore the wildness outdoors, for sweet voices called to her. She deeply felt their beguiling songs which seemed to invite her into their own special realm of being. But as the forest was full of prowling beasts and other unknown hazards, her parents would not abide the invitation. She must never wander from their sight.

One morning very early, something quite lovely happened. The gentle face of a young deer appeared up against the glass, and gazed at the princess with tender, wondering eyes. She returned his gaze, and who knows how long they remained this way; studying and measuring each other, searching out what lay developing in their young, wistful hearts?

The yearling came every day after that, and learned to communicate with the princess silently; for when heart speaks to heart, words only get in the way. The deer begged her to come out and dance with him in his own special meadow, and she, in turn, promised that someday, somehow, she would join him in his play and be his friend forever. Every day their bond grew stronger, in spite of the pane of glass between them, and the princess became quite determined to plunge into that world of pines, of mosses and deep silences that called to her so urgently.

In the meantime, sad things were happening in the castle. The queen had become quite ill, and despite the many doctors that poured in from all over the kingdom, she failed to improve. Even the local shamans with their strong herbal remedies were unsuccessful.

The queen grew weaker every day, until finally, one early spring evening, with her husband and young daughter beside her, she gave a gentle sigh, releasing her spirit from her body.

The king could not be comforted, and shut himself in his study for days on end, eating and drinking very little. When he finally emerged, thin and red-eyed, his jaw was firm, and his expression fierce. He set himself to many projects, and traveled around his kingdom for months at a time, returning only for a few days every month. Beyond establishing that she was well cared for, the king paid little attention to his lonely daughter.

Time passed, and the young girl learned how to be alone without being lonely. The servants, ensured the princess went to bed on time, was properly fed and clothed. But busy with their many jobs of castle keeping, paid little attention to her whereabouts the rest of the day.

Thus the princess, now in her teens, found herself free to roam and explore the natural beauty surrounding the castle as much as she pleased, wandering a little farther down hidden pathways every day. Her one disappointment was that her yearling friend, perhaps frightened away by the hubbub surrounding the queen's passing, no longer made his visits. She tried calling to him, but not recognizing voices, he never appeared.

Until one morning, following a new, faint trail flanked by elderly birch and white pine, she was startled by a soft nuzzling on the back of her neck. Turning, she saw none other than her old friend! He was much changed but recognizable by his deep brown eyes, carrying the same message of love that had shone through from outside the window. No longer a tender yearling, unsure of his place on earth, he was now a strong, wide-chested buck. The little knobby protrusions on the crown of his head had burst through their velvet and become a sturdy rack of antlers which the buck carried as proudly as any king. He spoke to her in their familiar voice of the heart. "Come," he commanded, and the princess followed without question. Deeper and deeper into the scented forest, they strode, until they came to a sunny meadow dotted with daisies and bluebells, and filled with the songs of many nesting birds. It was here that he taught her his dance of joy, and they pranced and whirled together with the lightest of steps until they tired, and lay down together to doze in the afternoon sun.

Afterwards, the buck led her to a splendidly sparkling brook where the princess drank deeply and ate a profusion of berries that grew along the banks. Nothing had ever tasted so sweet. Nothing had ever felt so like home. Her elegant stone-walled castle had been her prison all along.

Thus, the princess remained in the forest, and with the help of her friend, learned its ways. He taught her where the non-poisonous mushrooms grew and how to feast on turtle eggs without taking them all. He showed her where the wild asparagus flourished, and what kind of roots were tender and tasty enough for her to enjoy. She missed nothing from civilization.

In time, her friend introduced her to his family. The dainty doe was shy, and at first hid behind a birch tree, peering around it with a mixture of awe and curiosity. Her two spotted fawns, however, who had not yet had a chance to encounter fear, bounded to the princess at once, and rubbed up against her legs, (wondering at the same time why she only had two of them). As the weeks passed, they all became the best of friends, and the princess entertained them with tales of the world outside the forest. The fawns were delighted with the stories but found them hard to believe. Why would anyone sleep within four walls and a roof, and eat their dinners from plates? Why would they travel in a box on wheels, pulled by horses, when they had perfectly good legs to carry them where they needed to go? Nevertheless, they were fascinated by these absurdities and constantly begged to hear more.

Time passed, although the princess no longer had any concept of time. She slept when darkness came, rose with the first light of the sun. She ate when she was hungry, and bathed in the brook when she felt sticky and itchy. When nights were cold, a kindly old grandfather bear allowed her to share his cave with him, and kept her warm against his thick coat of fur.

In the beginning, many search parties were sent to find the princess, but she had learned the forest art of becoming invisible. She wove soft green leaves together with vines that grew along the banks of the creek, and rubbed the oil of wintergreen leaves into her skin. In this way the groups often passed within feet of her, and even the dogs were not able to pick up her scent. Her memories of life within the castle were becoming as faint as dreams, and never, even when she caught glimpses of her father, was she tempted to return. Life within the dappled shade of the forest was the only one the princess cared to have. She even forgot her name, as names carried no meaning in her new existence.

One day, as she wandered near to the edge of the forest, the princess heard the strange sound of weeping. Drawing nearer, and crouching in a thicket, she saw her father, the king, sitting with his head in his hands, weeping tears down into his graying beard. "Oh, my darling daughter, where are you? Will I ever see you again?"

The heart of the princess ached for him, and she began to sing—a high, sweet sound that seemed to come from a silver flute somewhere high in the treetops. The king raised his head to listen, and as he did so, the silvery notes penetrated his aching heart. They soothed and comforted him, he felt new strength and purpose come into his life. As he arose, he stood taller and walked more firmly. Even the grey steaks in his beard began to fade. From that day on, the king devoted himself more and more to the welfare of his people, and they loved and trusted him completely. He sent out a decree that there was to be no hunting allowed in the surrounding forest and the people believed in his wisdom, so they found other wild places to catch their dinners and obeyed him without a murmur.

This is not to say that the king was not sad from time to time, but the princess could feel when those moods came upon him ,and would sing her healing flute songs from wherever she happened to be. Somehow, her father heard them no matter where he was, and learned to understand the unspoken words: "I am near, Father, we shall meet again someday in another time, and another place." The king was greatly comforted and learned to go about his business of the day with patience and understanding, knowing that truth will mend and restore all lost joys when the time is right.

The forest was now free to follow the laws of nature, without interference from Man. The trees grew tall and sturdy until their sap ran slowly and they had passed their prime. Then, unable to withstand the pressure of fierce spring storms, the trees might topple to the forest floor where they would slowly return the nourishment which had fed them for so many years.

Underground, vast fungal networks wove tapestries, connecting entire root systems for a hundred miles or more, and exchanging nutrients within the forest's special barter system.

The animals flourished as well, free from the fear of sudden gun shots or arrows. The weak or the unwary were still prey for the hungry, but that is within forest law, and has always been so. Harsh rules, perhaps, but fair and easily understood. All was in its proper place.

The princess and the stag remained close for many years, and she watched, and made friends with generations of his offspring. When his muzzle became white, and his joints too stiff to forage far for food, she would bring him handfuls of berries and fresh water from the brook. One day she found him lying down, unable to rise. She knelt and cradled his head in her arms. "Don't cry, my dearest friend," he murmured, "my body must wear out in order to set my spirit free. I shall never be far from you, and we shall meet each other again in another realm." He closed his eyes, and the princess felt a soft, fragrant breeze, as his soul floated away through the treetops.

Her heart was full of sorrow, but she managed to carry him to his favorite meadow, where she laid him down on a grassy knoll surrounded by bluebells. There, she sang him a new song, one filled with all the love they had had for each other over the years.
Accompanied by the low hum of the honeybees, it was more beautiful than any she had ever sung, and the entire forest hushed itself to listen. In this way, she found that she had comforted herself, and thus, she also

knew that she could continue her life, wild and free as ever, knowing that endings are only beginnings.

Much later, when the time came for her to leave her own body behind, the now elderly princess remembered what her friend had told her, and eagerly lay down to await their reunion. Gentle hands gathered her up, and strains of her own flute songs surrounded her as she drifted off to begin another cycle of being.

To her great delight, the first to greet the princess when she reached her destination was her father, young and strong again with a merry look in his eyes. As the king gathered her into his arms, she felt a familiar nuzzle on her neck,
and turning, saw her oldest friend, once again a yearling, prancing with joy at the prospect of taking up life at her side once again. So, the bond that held the three together these many years had never been broken, only stretched out a bit,
only waiting for them all to find a common purpose: the three became the guardians of the forest. It became even lovelier than before, and such a mysterious sense of peace that the people of the kingdom called it "the Enchanted Forest," and no one found their way into it except the pure of heart.

These individuals found paths lined with the softest of green mosses, with all underbrush retreating to the edges. They were welcomed by the birds and all manner of wild things and were never allowed to be lost or frightened in the dark.

On the other hand, those who tried to enter with the gold of the outside world still gleaming in their eyes, and greedy purpose in their hearts, found the way barred with thickets of nettles, and large boulders dropped suddenly into their paths. Instead of birdsong, there were low, menacing wolf growls, and a sky darkened with thunder clouds. They would retreat, shuddering, and never try to breach the boundaries again.

And so, the forest became a haven of peace, serenity, and almost magical beauty, watched over by the faithful three. For, as we all should know by this time, it is only love and kindness, guided by wise hearts, that will allow our planet to remain safely within its orbit, and only by listening carefully to the whispers of our spirit guardians, will we be counted among the pure of heart.

A Doll for Ida

It was 1938, and I didn't know much about the world or life in general. However, having newly arrived from the city into this charming, old fashioned suburb, I did know there were a lot of things I loved. I loved the deep green lawns and the spreading trees that left their dappled shadow patterns across the streets. I loved the purple lilacs that, in the spring rains, sent their fragrance throughout the entire town. I loved roller skates, and the little library that was close enough for me to walk to all by myself. Most of all, I loved the simple freedom of an open front door, wide open to all the possibilities of a sunny Saturday morning.

And then there was Ida. She was the only black (colored was the term we used in those days) person I had ever met. Ida was our cook and general housekeeper, although my mother worked along side her a good deal of the time. When I came home from school, I could hear Ida chatting with my mother murmuring together in the kitchen as they began preparing dinner. "Them beans ain't as fresh as last time … Ah don't think I likes that new store much. Maybe they don't charge as much, but their food stuffs ain't all that good." "Yes, Maybe we'll go back to Bono's. They deliver too which makes things easier."

The A&P was a new arrival in town, as chain stores were beginning to spring up all over the country.

Everyone was fascinated with the shiny cleanness of its windows, and the seemingly endless supply of edibles displayed up and down its wide aisles. In contrast, Bono's was small, dark, old, and looked worn to death with the effort required to remain upright through its 70 plus years of business. However, Mr. Bono was everyone's good friend, and anything he didn't have in stock, he was happy to procure, and quickly too. I listened to this discussion, and decided I too preferred Bono's because he always handed me a green lollipop when I went in with Ida. I didn't completely cross the A&P off my list, though, because they had that lovely white processed bread that scrunched itself beautifully into hard little balls that I could throw at my brother when no one was looking.

Back to Ida, though, who is the real reason I am writing any of this. Ida, who in one summer afternoon, gave me a glimpse of an entirely different world apart from this pleasant little town, one I never imagined existed, and one I could never quite put out of my mind. One that would come back to me from time to time through many long years, and although I took no part in creating it, fills me with a heavy sense of guilt to this day. How I wish I could have found a way to buy her that doll! How I wish I had even thought of it back then!

I didn't know how old Ida was—none of us did because she wasn't telling. Maybe she didn't know herself. She had grey hair, though, all matted together like a bunch of Brillo pads.   She had no wrinkles, held herself erect, and moved quickly and efficiently. There was something about her that made age seem quite beside the point. To me, her most outstanding feature was a large, round mole on the edge of her nose, raised up and teetering there as if one good tweak would dislodge it. I'm afraid I spent much more time staring at it than was at all proper, but if she noticed my rudeness, she never gave any sign of it. Ida seldom laughed, or even smiled, but there was a calm dignity, a sense of peace about her that made me want to be near her. She was never fidgety or cross the way my mother sometimes was and I loved to sit with her in the kitchen and help knead bread or shell peas. It was a relaxing thing to do after what was often a hectic or perplexing day at school (I thought mastering long division was going to end up killing me). I now know that what seemed like peace and calm in Ida was more like resignation. I have come across it a number of times when confronted with persistent poverty.

One Saturday my mother informed me that Ida had invited my cousin and best friend, Nancy Ellen, and me to travel to the South Side with her for lunch at her home and a movie. We were excited, not because lunch with Ida seemed like anything special, but because it meant over an hour long trip on that remarkable method of transportation known simply as the El. The El (short for elevated, of course) was a train raised 30 feet or so above the ground, that hurtled around the business district of Chicago at breakneck speed and then headed down to the South Side for miles and miles, giving a view of the city not to be seen in any other manner. It rattled and roared a few feet away from thousands of brightly lit kitchen windows, giving sudden and brief visions of strangers within a crazy quilt of the city's backside.

The occupants of these window scenes were evidently so accustomed to being gaped at by strangers for all of 10 seconds that no one paid any attention, or bothered to draw a curtain. We would see a beer-drinking man in his undershirt, a woman, Medusa like in metal curlers standing at her stove, or two children playing a board game. Now and then a dog would race to the window to bark wildly and uselessly. Everything vanished so quickly that we retained no conscious memories, but the whole panoply seemed to leave photographic images all smashed up behind our eyelids. We were slightly dizzy and excited by the time our journey was over.

Once our feet were on solid ground again, we were greeted with a landscape that, in our young, carefully sheltered lives, we could never have believed existed. What was this place? Did real people actually live here? And why did they live here? I suppose we were at the age where it hadn't yet dawned on us that there were people in the world, even people we might know, that had very little choice about any aspect of their lives, let alone where they lived.

The first thing we noticed was the air. It smelled sharp and metallic with an undertone of something rotten, and in the sudden winds for which Chicago is famous, it seemed to rise up in attack mode and pepper our cheeks with tiny fragments of grit. If we opened our mouths, we could taste it. Even the sky, a brilliant August blue when we left home, had turned dull and pale grey with the poor sun struggling to shine through. The streets had strange, ragged holes irregularly scattered, and on the sidewalks, no two paving blocks were the same height. "No one could ever roller skate here," I thought. In the corners, and along the sagging chain link fences were collections of wadded up newspapers, broken bottles, rusty tin cans with their with labels long gone, and what seemed to be an inordinate number of torn, ragged sneakers of the same grim color as the sky. The buildings themselves were wooden, and if they had been painted at any time in the past, there were very few signs of it now. The entire area had a forgotten, "don't give a damn" aspect, and it was hard not to sink into the same dejected mood. We surreptitiously poked ourselves, "what are we getting into … ?"

The entrance to Ida's building didn't give us much cause for hope. The hallway was so dimly lit, that we could hardly see where to put our feet. When I complained, Ida answered with cheerful irony, "Be glad we got any light at all. Sometimes we just stumble around in the dark and maybe trip on a rat. Don't step on that third stair now, cause its broke." I remember the trip up to the third floor where Ida lived as rather terrifying, what with the strange, garbage-y smells, and the faint scuttling sound along the walls. In my mind I saw enormous rats with bared teeth just waiting to dig into my ankle. After this unpromising beginning, I hadn't much hope for what awaited us at the top of the stairs. When Ida opened her door, and we stood on the threshold, it reminds me now of Dorothy standing in the open door of her grim little shack and confronting the wonders of Munchkin land, all light and color. Bright light flooded the room, and starched white curtains hung crisply at the windows. The floor was a vividly patterned linoleum and here and there were a few green plants looking well-watered and cared for. The sparse furniture may have been shabby, and maybe there were cracks in the walls, but the whole atmosphere was one of kindly welcome and tender care. We hurried in gratefully and took deep breaths of the clean air. This is the Ida we knew, not the one moving through forsaken streets like a skinny, stray cat.

Ida set two chairs out on the fire escape for us to wait in while she fixed lunch. In a small courtyard below, a group of children were playing dodgeball with great hilarity and I remember thinking with surprise,

"Why, they're just like us!" A door opened into my automatic, and perhaps instinctive, racial prejudice and I was confronted head on with the national systemic problem that was not going to change any time soon. None of this really came through to me on this day, but something relaxed in me at the sight of so many children having plain, simple fun in spite of the unwelcoming surroundings. I had a strong compulsion to scramble down those rickety iron stairs and ask that one simple question we asked to open the gate to fun times: "Can I play too?" But of course I just stayed where I was and continued watching wistfully. Nancy Ellen didn't have the same somewhat reckless sense of adventure that often sent me off into the unknown. But more simply I was held back by my terror of fire escapes.

Something about looking straight through those flimsy iron bars to the ground below made me freeze, and I would be quite unable to move forward, remaining stuck in place, clinging desperately to the hand rail. This made me very unpopular during school fire drills with everyone piling up behind me shouting, "Move! Move!"

Ida made our favorite egg salad sandwiches for lunch, and even more delightfully, made on store-bought bread, nice and cottony. It occurs to me now that in her six day work week at our house, she didn't have time left over to make bread for her own family. Yes, there was a husband around somewhere named Bill, but I don't remember ever meeting him, and he was nowhere in sight that particular day. I have the feeling, as I recall the look of her apartment that day, that he did not play a very important role in Ida's life.

The movie theater was not far down the street, but we almost missed the beginning because our eyes were caught by an unexpected bit of wonder. Next to the theater, in a small building as dilapidated as the rest, we spied a window full of cheap, unappealing playthings, designed to be affordable to those who might have a dollar or two left over at the end of the week. But in the middle of this display on a dais, was an extraordinarily lovely doll. She stood about two feet high, dominating over the tawdry little scene at her feet like a queen, wearing a blue silk dress and bonnet to match. On her feet were white kid shoes with straps and lace-trimmed socks. She gazed out through the fly-specked window at the three of us with a dimpled smile, as if she were welcoming visitors to her kingdom. But far and above this magnificence was the dominating and surprising fact that her skin color was a deep creamy cocoa. None of us had ever seen a doll of color before, let alone a doll of this elegance, and we lingered in appreciation; and in Ida's case, pure awe. In fact, she stood gazing for so long that we feared missing the movie altogether. "Come on, Ida, we're late. Let's go." We whined, tugging at her hands. Reluctantly, she let us pull her away.

I have no recollection of the movie, or of the journey back to our green, leafy suburb. But I do remember that Ida wanted one more stop at the toy store window where she gazed again with deep longing in her eyes. I now imagine her thinking, "How I would have loved to have a doll like that when I was a little girl!" How any little girl would have loved to have a doll like that!

I haven't a very clear idea what the afterlife might be, but I have no doubt that there is one. Maybe not with pearly gates, and angels with harps, but something to help us make sense of what Shakespeare called "this naughty world." Somewhere in the middle of the Episcopal funeral service is the dreary pronouncement, "As you came into this world with nothing, so it is certain you can take nothing out of it." Really ... no exceptions? Anyway, I know that if by some curious bending of the rules, in that liminal space between life and death, that if a celestial being should offer me the opportunity of choosing one thing to bring along on the trip, I wouldn't have to think twice. I would tuck that wonderful doll under my arm and bring it straight to Ida, in whatever corner of the kingdom of God she may be resting. Too late, you may say—and you have a point. Even good deeds have a "sell by" date. Nevertheless, as I look back, I can see that a number of the things I have done, and a number of my viewpoints have been deeply affected by this memory of some 85 years ago. If every child in the world could have perhaps one truly lovely possession to remember—a bright red 10 speed bike, or a doll in a blue silk dress, would it not give them that sliver of hope, that patch of blue sky, that all of us need to keep plugging on? For in the grimy vortex of murdered dreams, hate is born … and love dies. Could Ida's doll just possibly make a difference somehow, somewhere, to someone? I don't really know, but I do know that we should all live our lives as if it would make all the difference in the world.

www.ingramcontent.com/pod-product-compliance
Lightning Source LLC
Chambersburg PA
CBHW050442150626
46551CB00028B/1126